X. J. Kennedy

EMILY DICKINSON
IN
SOUTHERN
CALIFORNIA

David R. Godine

FOR DOROTHY

David R. Godine Publisher
Boston, Massachusetts

LCC 73-81065

ISBN 0-87923-077-0

The wood engraving on the title page is by
Michael McCurdy

Designed by Carol Shloss

Number 1 in the
FIRST GODINE POETRY
CHAPBOOK SERIES

Jan Schreiber, General Editor

Emily Dickinson
in Southern California

Mining Town

Sheds for machines that lower tons of men
Clasp dirt for dear life. Clapboard houses lose
Gray clapboards the way a dying oak sheds bark.
One house they tell of plunged
Nose-down into a shaft last year with cries
Of people waking, falling.

Like boys in sneakers testing limber ice,
Gas stations growing bold now inch up near.
Who ever thinks that Kitchen Kounter World
Straddles pit One? Thick coaloil-colored clouds
Graze to the west.

It takes a while to learn to sleep on edge,
Always on edge, these townsmen like their trees
Locked to the wind's steep angle. When fear tells
It tells out of the corner of an eye,
A rickety house balancing in uncertainty.

Schizophrenic Girl

Having crept out this far,
So close your breath casts moisture on the pane,
Your eyes blank lenses opening part way
To the dead moonmoth fixed on pins of rain,
Why hover
A swimmer not quite surfaced, inches down
Fluttering water, making up her mind
To breathe, or drown?

All autumn, earth locked deeper in her slant
Back from the level sunlight, you, you wouldn't quit
That strait-backed chair we'd dress you in, you'd sit,
Petrified fire, casting a glare,
Refuse to swallow, to concede
There were such things as spoons. And so we'd feed
You through a vein
Smashed into like a lake we'd icefish in –
Can no one goad
You forth into the unsteady hearthlight of the sane?

Already, yawning child
At a dull drawn-out adult affair,
You whimper for permission to retire
To your room where black
T-squared shadows lie, vacuity
A sheet drawn halfway back.

If you'd just cry. Involved
Around some fixed point we can't see, you whirl
In a perpetual free-fall.
Turn back. We cannot stand
To see transformed to stone what had been hand,
What had been mind smoothed to a bright steel ball.

Evening Tide

Darkness invades the shallows of the street.
A tricycle left outdoors starts nodding and bobbing.

On its recliner by dusk set afloat
Father's head lolls, its dome of beer half-emptied.

Under the parked car in the driveway, shadows seep
And somewhere the cry of a child protesting bed
Comes blundering in again and again, a stick of driftwood.

Last Child

for Daniel

Small vampire, gorger at your mother's teat,
Dubious claim I didn't know I'd staked,
Like boomerangs your cries reverberate
Till roused half-blind, I bear you to be slaked,
Your step-and-fetch-it pimp.
                          Fat lot you care
If meadows fall before your trash-attack,
Streams go to ruin, waste be laid to air.
Will yours be that last straw that breaks earth's back?

Your fingers writhe: inane anemones
A decent ocean ought to starve. Instead
I hold you, I make tries at a caress.
You should not be. I cannot wish you dead.

Two Views of Rime and Meter

1

What's meter
but the thud
  thud
  thud of a bent wire
carpetbeater

fogging the air
with boredom
in dull time

and the dust,
rime?

2

Meter
Is the thrust rest thrust of loins and peter
And rime,
To come at the same time.

At Colonus

STRANGER: That was a sacred altar!
        You plant your buttocks there!

OEDIPUS: Where gods no more set table
        May not man make his chair?

Japanese Beetles

1

Imperious Muse, your arrows ever strike
When there's some urgent duty I dislike.

2

By the cold glow that lit my husband's eye
I could read what page eight had said to try.

3

To Someone Who Insisted I Look Up Someone

I rang them up while touring Timbuctoo,
Those bosom chums to whom you're known as '*Who?*'

4

Parody: Herrick

When Vestalina's thin white hand cuts cheese
The very mice go down upon their knees.

5

The Minotaur's Advice

Unravel hope, but be not by it led,
Or back outside you shall hang by a thread.

6

On his wife's stone, though small in cost and small,
Meek got a word in edgewise after all.

7

Translator

They say he knows, who renders Old High Dutch,
His own tongue only, and of it not much.

8
To a Now-type Poet

Your stoned head's least whim jotted down white-hot?
Enough confusion of my own, I've got.

9
At a Sale of Manuscript

Who deal in early drafts and casual words
Would starve the horse to death and prize his turds.

10
To a Young Poet

On solemn asses fall plush sinecures,
So keep a straight face and sit tight on yours.

Last Lines

From the Greek Anthology

On miserable Nearchos' bones lie lightly, earth,
That the dogs may dig him up, for what he's worth.

2
On a Boxer

In his still corner Rocky takes the count.
He would not rise again for any amount.

3

Full-nelsoned in earth's arms the Crusher sleeps
Whom no man living could pin down for keeps.

4
Teutonic Scholar

Whose views twelve heavy tomes perpetuate
Now lies as though beneath a paperweight.

5

Here lies a girl whose beauty made Time stay.
Shovel earth in. We haven't got all day.

A Little Night Music

Fingers undo the taut
Peg of a thighbone, chin
Takes hold, bow draws a light
Test cry from violin.

In love we tune for death,
So if you're not averse,
My dear, undress. In bed
We'll dress-rehearse the hearse.

Crawfish

after Apollinaire

Uncertainty O my secret joy
To make tracks you and I
Must turn tail like the craw
And withdraw and withdraw

Bells

after Apollinaire

Wanderin' man my lover
Keep still the churchbells sound
In deep each other we got lost
Not dreaming we'd be found

But we weren't even covered up
Now all the bells have spied
Our secret from their steepletops
And spilled it villagewide

Tomorrow Cyprien and Henri
Catherine and Marie-Ursule
The baker's wife the baker
And Cousin Gertrude all

Will smile at me when I go by
I won't know where to lay me
You'll be far from my side I'll cry
And that will kill me
                maybe

Onan's Soliloquy

She'll none of me?
                 Like hell. She's mine alone.
Self-ordained priest, I elevate my bone.
Or else: behind locked eyes behold her bust
Projected wobbling on a screen of dust,
Skim her clitoris's pert dot of braille,
Led by my German shepherd round her tail,
Fumble her dim unconscionable tits –

Darkness all mine for lover. And I its.

Emily Dickinson in Southern California

1

I called one day – on Eden's strand
But did not find her – Home –
Surfboarders triumphed in – in Waves –
Archangels of the Foam –

I walked a pace – I tripped across
Browned couples – in cahoots –
No more than Tides need shells to fill
Did they need – bathing suits –

From low boughs – that the Sun kist – hung
A Fruit to taste – at will –
October rustled but – Mankind
Seemed elsewhere gone – to Fall –

2

The Tour Boat hurtles – Newport Bay –
Till I go by – in flood –
An Island – Jimmy Cagney won –
One night – at high card stud –

And genuflecting to a Breeze –
White-bosomed Schooners – dodge –
Obeisant as Gondolas
Before a passing Doge –

I spy the House – that King Gillette
Whom Whiskers – had enthroned –
Built Wings so wide – they quite sliced off
His nextdoor Brother's – sun –

And prickling as it chills – the Bay
Beholds a Full Moon rise
That – squeezing earthward through a Lens
Of Smog – Immensifies –

3

There is a habitude – of Sound –
Intrinsic – to the Skull –
To keep a Measure stalking – though
Pendulums – stand still –

How Oversized – the fallen Hush –
It takes a whittling Ear
To shave it to a Point – and push
Hard through – till One – not hear –

4

When Hopelessness – moved in with me –
He brought a ball of Twine
And wrapped it three times – round my heart –
To keep my heart – in line –

And every time my heart – thrashed up –
He'd jerk back till – each Valve
Drew shut and – reined there – flittering –
I'd watch the Light – dissolve –

And then he'd whisper – me in Hand –
'Dear little sister – how
Can you wish other – than this Earth
And all its Goods?' – And now –

Content to peck – his bitter Grits –
It sits here – being His –
And would no longer dream – to Soar –
For all the Sky – there is –

5

I wrote all night – till break of Mind –
Tongue thick – teeth clogged with Sludge –
What decent words – were there to find?
'Oh flab!' – 'Ah freeby fudge!'

Some days you can't – do more than cant –
My old White Owl died out –
Then – Universe stood up in me
To take a sharper – squint –

Impatient Lepers – queued for miles –
A split-hair more – thought-free –
And – I had healed 'em! Out winked – I –
And what was left but – me –

6

I took my Spirit – for a walk –
A scabbed Thing – and a scaled –
Tongued with the flicker of a Snake
And Alligator-tailed –

Its Belly – grated raw the Ground –
Its mailed Feet marched in rows –
Down to the thick black Lily pond
I drove it – it nosed ooze –

And – thirsting – lunged as some Toad would –
And bubbled out of sight –
The wasted Sun sat down – I stood –
The Dark leapt bolt upright –

And held me – clenched – I couldn't breathe
One Pulsebeat more – when out
That Beast broke! Like a Blizzard banked –
White Lilies wreathed its Snout –

7

The Storm came home too blind to stand –
He thwacked down Oaks like chairs –
Shattered a Lake and – in the dark –
Head over heels downstairs
Rolled – and up grumbling on his knees
Made nine white tries to scratch
Against Walls – that kept billowing –
The strict head of his Match –

8

I'm loath to tolerate a Sky
That will not stand for Storm –
As Ceiling were to militate
Against Sound in its Room –

The Concord orchard Macintosh –
Wart-cheeked and bubble-chinned –
Has freckles like an Aunt you'd trust
And handclasp – like a Friend –

But gazing at the Fresno – Grape –
Of sleek perfectioned Jaw –
I fear the Planet should gape wide –
Did One discern its Flaw –

9

I bore Hope's candle farthest West –
And now – obliged to halt –
Hear Asia's rumor of despair
Behind a wall of Salt –

Categories

Nothing stays put: the copra-eating apes
Drop from their trees and switch to centipedes,
Species collide like too-close-following cars,
Infants cut teeth, no sooner is the course
In Post-Arnoldian Prose Style dittoed up
Than styles expire, essential stylists change
Sexes or nations. On the strand
Vast mollusks punch-drunk from the surf relax,
Molt butterflies.

The century clots, or thoughtlessly as sand,
Collapses through the mind's pained hourglass.
Was it Rimbaud, that trader of tusks, who said
No man begins to understand
Till through the tip of his tongue he hear bright red?
Was it that master in Kyoto who began
To seize on what had been left out before
When one of the novice monks, a scrubber of pots,
Demonstrated that you can,
If you have hatched from names, or lack clean plates,
Serve cake on a shut fan?

Salute Sweet Deceptions

Salute sweet deceptions!
In wannest morning
How the brick firehouse
Seems hewn from amber,

How flung-in beercans
Mime stars dissolving,
A seedpearl necklace
Of rain wears phonewires.

To an Angry God

Lend me cruel light
That, reading over words I write,
I do not skim forgivingly. Not spare,
But smite.

Protest

On marble stairs under the bloated dome of time
Everyone living sets himself on fire.

Some of these poems, as they are now or in earlier versions, first appeared in *Antæus, Arbor, The Back Door, Boston Review of the Arts, Concerning Poetry, Dare, Hearse, Michigan Quarterly Review, The New York Times, Open Places, Renaissance, Southern Poetry Review, Spirit,* and *West Coast Review.* Thanks to the editors concerned. Apollinaire's 'Crawfish' was first published in *Poems from France* edited by William Jay Smith (New York: Thomas Y. Crowell, 1967). 'To Someone Who Insisted I Look Up Someone' (now one of the 'Japanese Beetles') first appeared in *Pith and Vinegar* edited by William Cole (New York: Simon and Schuster, 1969). Other versions of 'Last Child' and 'Japanese Beetles' appeared in the author's *Breaking and Entering* (London: Oxford University Press, 1971). 'At Colonus' was first published in *Poetry.* 'When Hopelessness moved in with me,' now part of 'Emily Dickinson in Southern California,' was copyright 1964 by *Shenandoah: The Washington and Lee University Review,* and is reprinted by permission of the editor.